The Creative Word

The Creative Word

The Young Child's Experience of Language and Stories

Daniel Udo de Haes

WECAN

WALDORF EARLY CHILDHOOD
ASSOCIATION OF NORTH AMERICA

The Creative Word:
The Young Child's Experience of Language and Stories
© 2014 Waldorf Early Childhood Association of North America

This book was originally published in 1972 in Dutch as *Van peuter tot kleuter—het kleine kind voor de sprookjesleeftijd.* An English translation was published in 1986 by Floris Books as *The Young Child: Creative Living with Two-to-Four-Year-Olds.* The translation by Simon and Paulamaria Blaxland deLange was revised for this edition by Lory Widmer.

Cover photo by Igor Yaruta (123RF.com)
Book design by Lory Widmer

ISBN: 978-1-936849-24-6

This publication was made possible by a grant
from the Waldorf Curriculum Fund.

WECAN
WALDORF EARLY CHILDHOOD
ASSOCIATION OF NORTH AMERICA

Waldorf Early Childhood Association of North America
285 Hungry Hollow Rd. Spring Valley, NY 10977
845-352-1690 / info@waldorfearlychildhood.org
www.waldorfearlychildhood.org

For a complete book catalog,
contact WECAN or visit our online store:
store.waldorfearlychildhood.org

Contents

Note to the WECAN edition

This book was first published in 1972 in Dutch as *Van peuter tot kleuter—het kleine kind voor de sprookjesleeftijd*, which could be translated as "From Toddler to Young Child—The Age before Fairy Tales." It was later translated into English and published by Floris Books as *The Young Child: Creative Living with Two-to-Four-Year-Olds*. The title of our new WECAN edition, *The Creative Word: The Young Child's Experience of Language and Stories* again includes the reference to the child's experiences of the creative word, first through the direct encounter with nature and later through the richness of nursery rhymes, picture books, and simple stories.

This book has been a much-appreciated resource for Waldorf early childhood educators, especially those working with toddlers and nursery or pre-school children, and for parents who are seeking to accompany their young children's language development with sensitivity and creativity. We are very pleased to be able to make it possible for Daniel Udo de Haes's rich insights and observations to reach a new generation of readers.

—*Susan Howard, WECAN Coordinator*

1 First sense impressions

When we see a two-year-old playing with a ball, we may be struck by how differently he or she plays from children of any other age, even those only a little older. Grown-ups and also older children throw, hit, or kick* the ball through a definite goal; schoolchildren pat and bounce it; the child of kindergarten age throws it and tries to catch it again—but the very young child does something altogether different. While what matters to the older children and adults is what is *done with* the ball, a toddler, as we may see, is completely absorbed in the ball itself. She sees its heavenly round shape, she lets it roll and runs after it, she observes its colors; and if it is a woolen or patchwork ball she will touch and cuddle it and does not grow weary of what it has to offer her.

Thus the toddler observes with an utterly open soul not only the ball, but all other objects and also all that happens and is done around her; and when we see how completely she is absorbed in this, we are bound to feel how important these early sense-impressions—and her deep inner experiences—must be for her. This quiet activity, which takes place behind her dreaming, wondering, or delighted eyes, remains hidden to us. Our adult consciousness has lost the connection with what goes on in the dreamy depths of the child's soul. But we may be able to sense how little children, who are still so close to the spirit-land whence they came, can still see something of the cosmic, and sometimes also the moral, source of the things in their surroundings; and that they can still experience something of that region which *we* can only grope towards with our thoughts.

But these profoundly moral experiences of very young children are by no means confined to those things which still speak naturally to us—for, as we saw in the case of the ball, even the most ordinary things which surround them reveal their hidden picture-language. Consider a cupboard, for example. Little children are still able to perceive, in their own way, that the cupboard (especially of course the toy-cupboard!) represents the quiet guarding of secrets, while through the bowl or plate they experience, by contrast, a willingness to give away, quite openly and unselfishly, the most valuable things.

Again, a child may see how his mother makes the precious dough flow into form, and he feels to the depths of his being that his own inner treasures have to be molded into earthly form, have to be embodied. And if then he sees the dough rise in the warm oven, may we not imagine this miracle taking place also within him? For everything from the heights of heaven which has adopted tangible form in him must now in this embodiment surely also rise, cherished by the love of parents and others.

In this way we could continue to make ourselves aware of the elementary "soul-language" through which children's surroundings speak to them especially in this toddler stage—a language which they still dreamily absorb in its full depth and intensity.

Even wider circles of people are becoming interested in the profound wisdom which the old folk tales express through their colorful images,** and many can feel something of their deep origin and of the great, but veiled, beacons on life's path which they present to children of kindergarten age. But few can listen with the very youngest children to the still more archetypal picture-language of the things in their surroundings, which touches more deeply the life that slumbers in the soul. Now, however, the time has come when we must, for our children's sake, understand also these deep secrets which our surroundings whisper to every still listener. It is an understanding that must be found not with our intellect alone, but with a part of our own inner soul-life, as the toddler still does fully.

When we learn to enter even a little into these first soul-experiences, it will become clear to us how vast this language is which addresses young children before they learn to understand ours. Then we realize that toddlers cannot yet be receptive to fairy-tales, for instance, and that this is not only because certain capacities, such as vocabulary and ability to follow the thread of the story, are insufficiently developed, but because they have a *faculty* which is still very much alive: they can listen to those even deeper messages, to the language of the things and actions themselves and also to the *sound* of human words, an ability which we have already lost. Toddlers still understand these archetypal revelations from their surroundings, and they will not allow themselves to be distracted by the more complex language of fairy-tales, or even our normal conceptual language.

How is it that the child's environment can impart such deep secrets, concerning even the very foundation of his own being? When we ask this question, we can make the strange discovery that the answer is given to us by the earth and by the child himself. Does not the whole of the visible and audible world originate from the same cosmic fount as the child's soul, and are not both an expression of this well-spring which lies at the foundation of all being? Here we may see clearly exemplified Goethe's maxim, that like can be perceived only by its like.

What could the ball tell a toddler, if she did not already bear something of its nature in herself? If the "memory" of the heavenly world and its perfection did not slumber within the child, and if it were not this same cosmic perfection that was manifested by the form and nature of the ball, what could the object mean to her? A *recognition* takes place in the child, dreamy yet profound, and thus the encounter with the ball, even for the first time, is more like a miraculous *reunion* than a meeting with something strange.

And if the child's soul were not itself a bearer of mysteries, how could an everyday object that also encloses mysteries, as the cupboard does, ever excite more than superficial curiosity? But even this ordinary object in daily use is recognized by the toddler—and also to some extent by us adults—as a symbol, and felt to be an outward manifestation of the mystery-bearing aspect of our own soul. Do we not speak of the shrine of the heart? The treasures that lie hidden in the heart of the child spring, however, from that same heavenly world from which the soul itself originated, and when this soul descends to earth, it finds that its rich possessions have miraculously reappeared around it.

When, in former times, men sought again for the world of spirit, they tried to open their souls as fully as possible to the lofty world of the gods by offering a sacrifice. If it was brought to the gods in a chalice, the openness of the chalice could reflect the soul's eagerness to lay itself bare to the gods—for there was, on the one hand, a deep inner longing to be at one with the higher powers, and, on the other, a hope of receiving their blessing. The soul itself can be an open chalice which offers its most treasured secrets to the divine and at the same time hopes to receive life-giving forces.

Young children, although much more open and receptive vessels than we are, are of course not yet capable of offering a sacrifice. They give to us richly, though not yet consciously, of themselves, but while the soul is on the path of descent sacrifices cannot yet have any meaning for young children. They do feel, though, that faculties slumbering within them are being addressed through the open giving and receiving that is manifested by the dish or plate in ordinary life.

One more recognition experience is that of the gate. With all these experiences we have been concerned with the relationship between the two soul-realms of the child: that of the earthly world, and that of the spirit which contains the archetypal origins of earthly objects. The soul of the child moves incessantly from one to the other. This heavenly gate through which all children have to pass again and again is represented in each earthly door or gate which leads from one space into another. These gates or doors on earth touch the deeply hidden memory of the heavenly gate through which the child's soul can still pass at any moment.

Even adults still experience something of this memory; for us, too, this heavenly gate still exists. But there are two differences between the child and ourselves in this respect.

The first is that we, as inhabitants of the earth, have to search again for our connection with the spirit—in other words, we try to pass through this gate on an ascending path, while the child moves from the heavens to the earth in a descending direction. This is expressed in the departure from earthly life, when we speak of "passing through the gate of death." For the little child the descent of the soul through heaven's gate to the earth does not only take place at physical birth; it is a process that begins long before and continues for a long time afterwards, as Wordsworth expressed in his ode, "Intimations of Immortality":

Our birth is but a sleep and a forgetting:
The soul that rises with us, our life's star,
Hath had elsewhere its setting,
And cometh from afar;
Not in entire forgetfulness,
And not in utter nakedness,
But trailing clouds of glory do we come
From God who is our home.

The second great difference is that, whereas the gate through which we have to pass if we seek to return to the spiritual world during our lifetime is generally tightly shut and difficult to open, for young children it is still quite open in both directions, though gradually closing as they grow older.

Shades of the prison-house begin to close
Upon the growing boy . . .

Even when young children are "awake," they can in a day-dreaming way still pass lightly to and fro at every moment and with each experience. For them, heaven and earth are still essentially one. The gate is always open.

How is it that children, who experience so deeply this inner relationship with their surroundings, can wonder so fervently at everything they perceive? Later we shall see that it is precisely this recognition which calls forth such wonder. It is the inner experience of wonder that we observe in young children as they marvel at the world.

In order to form a somewhat clearer picture, we could perhaps compare this "marveling at the familiar" with the surprise that we would feel if, upon arriving in a strange country, we were to meet only intimate friends who, oddly enough, were clad in native costume.

In the next chapter we shall give closer attention to this heavenly realm which is so very different. Allowing toddlers to be completely absorbed in their surroundings enables them to perceive archetypal images. So here we see—in its purest and most archetypal form—like being assimilated by its likeness.

Endnotes to Chapter 1

* There is no longer any feeling nowadays for what it means to kick an object, especially because of soccer, which has become so popular. When, however, we become aware that it is our legs that carry us about on earth and connect us with it, we shall be able to develop a sense of how coarse it is to kick something that is of the earth—and especially something that brings to expression on earth the form of the heavens, namely, the ball. Then it will also be clear that the coarsening effect of even observing this kicking will have a particular influence on the child. Personally, I am convinced that the crude effect of this sport, which has taken on such demagogic forms in our society today, is greater than most of us imagine.

** See, for instance Rudolf Meyer, *The Wisdom of Fairy Tales*, Floris Books, 1987.

2 | The two worlds of the child

Clearly, it will be meaningful to immerse ourselves in young children's experiences of their surroundings only if we try to awaken a vivid inner awareness that we, too, once bore within us the foundations of our soul-life from the spirit-land from whence we came.

In the child's environment, we discover two distinct realms. The first is the natural world, which in the home is present through pets, house plants, or the elements of earth, water, and so on; the second is the human realm, full of man-made things, which forms quite a considerable part of the world that surrounds us.

It is gratifying that many parents feel how important it is for children to be allowed to find an intimate relationship with the things around them. As far as nature is concerned, consider, for instance, the substance with which children have such a special connection—water.

The ability of the child to live in two worlds, which we described in the last chapter, has a close affinity to the life and nature of an amphibian, which lives both in water, its world of origin, and on dry land. This amphibious aspect of soul-life appears—more clearly in the toddler than in the child of kindergarten age—in all that the little one observes and experiences; but water is particularly important. What the little child can experience both in and with water is nearly limitless, and it is wholesome for children to play freely with water. With this attitude, we see the harm of scolding such as "Look now, what a mess you have made!"—which nullifies the joy and also the deeper effect of the play and makes children feel that they have done something "bad." Many parents now even consider such games as pottering about in the garden with water or with the mud of a rain-puddle to be a blessing for these little ones. Others will now and then give children a bowl of water so that even indoors they can play with this wet element to their heart's content. It can be a joy to see children absorbed in his play, and as its therapeutic value for their development comes to be more appreciated, it will be seen as an essential and matter-of-course part of the care and education of children.

As a second example, we may take the wonderful substance that combines the fluid properties of water and the hardness of earth—pure, white sand. We can rejoice in the adult who makes a small sandpit in the garden or even in the living room, where children can enjoy the forming and pouring of this wonderful substance.

In contrast to the sense for the substances of nature, a relationship with man-made objects helps children feel that their own journey from heaven to earth has already been accomplished by the whole of humanity and is still taking place. Where nature offers beacons which show the way, man-made things are signposts left by those that have gone before—and these also speak deeply to the child's soul. They can be the simplest things, large or small—for instance, little pieces of cloth of various colors (where not only the colors but also an enveloping quality may be experienced), or a bowl and spoon, or a bucket and spade, or a small jug or cup, and so on. With the bucket or cup, the importance lies in the image of taking-up and letting-go, receiving and giving away again of the precious substance contained in these man-made objects. This experience addresses moral qualities and aids in their unfolding.

In this larger human context we may return to two earlier examples, which have a twofold message to impart. The sphere or ball made by a human being, whether it be as ornament, plaything, or for some other purpose, not only speaks to toddlers' unbroken connection with the heavens, but can facilitate a dreamy absorption in the spiritual origin of all mankind.

In contrast, we may see how the adult whose soul has become a "shrine," and has made cupboards, or shrines, on earth, can show the way to children in their recapitulation of evolution. The child in search of individual selfhood can also feel a part of humanity as a whole. Older children, who to a certain extent have already gained their independence, like to have their own cupboards to keep their treasures and secrets.

In examining ordinary, man-made things like a table, a chair, a knife, a fork, a book, it will be seen that every object has, beyond the practical reasons for its existence, roots in a deeper reality—and these are experienced profoundly by the little child who observes the object and what it does. Of course, we are here considering only simple, elementary things, and not technologically complex objects, where the deeper reality is obscured and often less favorable.

We can understand why it is the most "everyday" manifestations, those we pass by without noticing, that so boundlessly enthrall our young children, who quietly behold what they disclose. For children to be able to call to life all the good that they bring from their heavenly home, and for these gifts to thrive, depends not only upon our loving and understanding care, but also on the quality of the surroundings in which they grow up.

3 Archetypal images

Children take a giant step when they move from a wonder-filled experience of the environment to absorption in the pictures of fairy-tales—in other words, when they are growing out of the toddler stage and beginning to tread the earth more firmly. This process must be guided with care, and must occur in its own time, neither too fast nor too early. To be able to follow the child through this transition, let us look a little closer at certain important themes.

Let us return to the earlier example of water, with its special, intimate fascination for people of all ages. Every human soul is aware, consciously or unconsciously, of a connection with this watery element. Does not each of us long for the clarity which pure water can manifest? Does not every soul feel its own ability to stream and flow in all directions, to wave and dash, to seethe and toss or to reflect calmly? Ultimately, the soul's capacity of rising to the heavens and descending again to earth is brought to expression by water. Little children experience all this much more directly and intensely than we do, though less consciously, and it is for this reason that they feel a connection with water and play with it with such abandon.

Our second theme is the "house," or "dwelling." We observe

how toddlers can be fascinated by a picture of a little house, how gladly children of kindergarten age will listen to stories about a little house or draw one themselves, and how they can be absorbed in building a little "house" out of the things in the room and in "living" in it. We become aware how deeply the archetype "house" lives in children's souls, and we may feel that what dwells there did not enter through first seeing houses or their construction, but was already present in the soul and simply awakened from slumber by these observations. In descending to earth, the soul bore within it the task of helping to build the "house" that it would have to live in during the life that was about to begin, for the task that it was assigned was to help in forming its body. We should therefore not be surprised at the joy with which children build a little house, thus symbolically fulfilling the task of building the body; nor should we be astonished at the great impression which each tale about a little house makes.

A third subject will lead us to a closer experience of this step that the child takes—and this we shall find if, through focusing upon our own being in its totality, we are confronted with *the human being*. Children in the cradle experience first the *people*, and only then, little by little, the *things* in their surroundings. So we may ask, how does the toddler experience the human being as such?

This may seem an abstract question, as our image of the human being is derived from sense perceptions, and is only to a very small degree an inner experience. With young children it is the other way around. Children do not as yet have any conscious picture of the human being, but in their souls this concept lives as a foundation for the whole of their development. Their souls continue to be vividly animated by this archetypal idea, *Human Being*, and from it they begin and continue to fashion their lives.

The existence of this deep foundation can often become evident through the close connection that some children feel with a doll, and through the way they give themselves up so totally to caring for this "baby." Naturally this playing with the doll stems partly from imitation, and there are also innate caring instincts which play their part (these can also assert themselves with a teddy bear, a kitten, or a puppy). Yet this does not alter the fact that in playing with the doll the child's soul addresses an image of the human being, and the process of incarnation and further development is quietly strengthened and deepened.

Children's firm connection with the human archetype can also come to expression through their drawings, and this we may see in particular through their frequent and characteristically childish representations (or rather indications) of the human form. We tend to dismiss this as "drawing little people." The truth is that such scribbling is not done as a trifling pastime but with complete dedication; for it springs from the impulse to bring to expression the archetypal idea of the human being.

Children experience something of this image—however unconsciously—in every person they meet; and if allowed scope for development, this can be very important in social life later on. Thus there is all the more reason for allowing free development of this treasure that the child's soul has brought from earliest childhood. This image of the human being will also play its part in the transition towards fairy-tales.

4 | The resonance of the soul

Two things stand as signposts pointing towards fairy-tales. The first concerns the being who brings children their first stories; the second concerns the moment at which fairy-tales in human language become possible, when we ourselves can begin to tell the children something.

Firstly, it is not the mother or grandmother, or even the teacher, who brings the first stories; this task is performed by none other than Mother Earth. For as we have seen, it is this greatest mother of all who tells us, in tales that may be read only by the dreamy soul of the child, that the source of all that surrounds us lies in the spiritual world.

The souls of young children resound with everything that Mother Earth "tells" them. This resonance originates in life before birth, and the child's mood of quiet wonder is, in fact, the deep reverberation of this prenatal sound.

We have tried to show how vibrantly these first inner chords of sympathy with the world resound within young children, and how tenderly these rudimentary dream-sounds enthrall them. In this dream-state the child feels the merging of the soul's wealth with what the senses offer; and through this uniting of "heaven and earth" the gate to earthly life is opened to what lives within the soul. Here children are offered the opportunity to incarnate healthily and to unfold their gifts in the course of life's journey.

It is understandable that we should not "interrupt" with other tales the picture-clad stories told by Mother Earth while they still speak so powerfully to the child. Therefore we should not introduce fairy-tales just yet, for, while these also have a heavenly origin, they bring in details and associations at a time when the child still experiences the archetypal elements.

To know when to begin with fairy-tales we must ask two questions: how intensely does the child still live in her surroundings and in what they tell her about the heavenly origin of the world; and, to what extent is it possible for her to open herself—without harming this capacity to "listen"—to what fairy-tales have to tell her? In other words, when can the child listen to what is said *about* the things around her without disturbing the intimate language which they *themselves* speak?

Finding a right answer requires a deep inner searching and an intimate sympathy with the child. As we pursue our question, we shall also include general considerations which may help us.

At one time or another everyone has been deeply moved by an experience of nature, whether it is an individual flower or a breath-taking landscape. We can feel, "What I now experience so deeply comes not only from outside me, but is also present within me; I have an inner resonance to my sense-impression. The true essence of what I observe stems from the world from which my soul also proceeds, and it is due to seeds that I already bear within me that I have been able to share in such a great experience."

There can be a similar feeling with a great work of art, or the saying of a great man or woman. Here again, like can be perceived only by like. As Goethe put it: "If God's own forces did not dwell within us, how could that which is God-like move us?" The sublime that is present within us in seed form can be wakened from its slumber by what is great in what we perceive. Every human soul can resound with the entire creation.

Now, in young children this resonance is strongest in meeting "ordinary" things and events. For them this is the "sublime," the "great" in the world, for these simple things, in their own *earthly* appearance, can speak to them in the language of their *heavenly* origin. Through this bridging capacity they unlock the passage from their world of origin—which is also the child's—to the life which he seeks on earth.

In these relationships we feel at once the deep affinity and the great difference between the young child and the adult. For each, in his own way and in his own realm, the earth-world is an expression of the spirit.

This clears the way for the child to bear heavenly gifts into earthly existence, while for the adult it represents an opportunity of rediscovering our spiritual home on earth. This we must regard as a matter of inner development, a task for a renewed spiritual life, which to a great extent is the meaning of our life on earth.

But the fulfillment of this adult task will be helped greatly where these spiritual seeds can be brought alive during early childhood. An adult will find it difficult to grasp that water, and with it also his own soul, has a heavenly origin, if he has not been able to feel at one with this substance when playing as a child. Only much later will aspects of life other than those introduced in earliest childhood remind the soul from whence it came, and also afford it a glimpse into the future; childhood experiences will bring a greater depth and vitality to these encounters. The importance of young children's experience of recognition extends through their whole life to come.

5 | The effect of fairy-tales on toddlers

As we follow the child's growth, we approach the world of fairy-tales, beginning with the shortest and simplest, and telling them in an open manner. How can we find the right moment to begin?

It goes without saying that we do not start telling stories before the child can follow a simple tale without difficulty. Often, however, whether out of enthusiasm for the fairy-tale, or through looking at a picture-book, we inadvertently make children follow our words before they are truly ready. We observed that one should not disturb Mother Earth as she tells the child of her wonders. What is the consequence if we "interrupt" her in telling her tale?

We turn our attention again to that substance with which the toddler is so deeply connected, namely water, and now imagine that while he is looking at a picture, we tell him about "enchanted water" and its powers. Enchanted water appears, for example, in Grimm's fairy-tale "Brother and Sister." Two children who are escaping from their angry stepmother enter a dark wood, where they find that all the springs have been charmed by her into changing everyone who drinks from them into an animal.

While we would never set out to tell this story to a toddler—
it is after all, very complicated and by no means easy even for
a five-year-old child—we might possibly find ourselves show-
ing a picture of the little brother drinking from one of these
springs and telling him of the consequences.

We might feel how the dramatic images in this tale, images
of the transformation of the little brother into an animal
and his deliverance from this condition, bring to expression
fundamental laws of development that work fruitfully and
formatively on the soul-life of the young child. But how will
a two- or three-year-old child experience first the enchanted
water and then its influence on the little brother?

We spoke earlier of how water, in all its movings and flow-
ings and in its potential clarity, presents, especially to young
children, a pictorial impression of the sources and stream-
ings of their own souls and of the hidden longing for inner
purity. We saw how children can be completely absorbed in
this substance, and how this helps them to "flow into" the
earthly world with all their inner wealth. Now suppose they
were to hear something about "enchanted" or "poisoned"
water, which changes whoever drinks it into an animal; and
that, furthermore, they see this outcome in a picture. They
would be greatly disturbed, and their whole relationship to
the wonderfully pure quality of water would be clouded and
even poisoned. The little brother's subsequent deliverance
from the spell cannot make this good, for with the toddler
we are concerned with *direct* sense-impressions, and the
thread of the story cannot as yet be followed. Moreover, the
enchantment and purifying of the water itself is not specifi-
cally mentioned in the fairy-tale; and so for the young child
the poison remains there.

Toddlers do of course hear the sounds that form the foundation of what an older brother or sister experiences in the fairy-tale. But as they are still unable to follow the story, the primary experience is for them wholly in the foreground, and the enchantment of the water works upon them, and is experienced in a negative way. From this we may see how harmful this sullied image of water's elemental purity may be for young children, even though the adult might not be aware of it.

Something similar can happen with the theme of "house" or "home." We described how the absorption of the child (both the toddler and the somewhat older child) in all that has to do with "home" and "living in a house" and "building a house" proceeds from his experience before birth of the task of building a "home" or "house" for the soul—of forming the body and going to live in it.

It will be clear that this theme of "home," which we may observe everywhere about us with our senses, is also one of the archetypal aspects of the child's own soul-life. It is therefore not surprising that it makes a deep impression if children are told in the fairy-tale of "Hansel and Gretel" about a little house which two children find in the dark wood where they have become lost. All that slumbers in the child's soul on the theme of "home" is being addressed here.

But now it is related of this little house that it consists entirely of cake and sugar-candy, and that when the children nibble this they fall into the hands of a witch who comes out of the house.

Again, profound realities of life are brought before us here. The bodily forces and substances are consumed through actions, emotions, and even thinking. The soul feeds off its body, which at night is repaired again and replenished. Here we can see that the growing consciousness, which is often quite clever and always stands in danger of becoming rather *too* clever, or even sly, is depicted as the treacherous inhabitant of the little house, the "witch," into whose power the soul falls when it allows itself to be tempted to eat of the little house (the body) in an irresponsible fashion—in other words, to "nibble" at it.

The child of fairy-tale age meets with deep truths here, which in this pictorial form are beacons for his own soul-life. The resolution that follows the overcoming of the witch and the rediscovering of the father's house (or "the house of the Father-God") holds the promise that his own development will be brought to a positive conclusion.

But the toddler still lives very sleepily in his "body-house," and scarcely "eats" or "nibbles" it at all; as yet, he hardly does anything but help to build this little house in dream or sleep, and there is in particular no sign of a witch-like inhabitant (the clever brain) emerging. This little one just lives utterly untroubled in the mystery "house," dreamily entering ever deeper into it, and as yet he does not become aware of any difficulties.

These fairy-tale images are of course even for the five- or six-year-old mostly themes for the future—but even so, a child of this age will not be disturbed by hearing them, as happens with the toddler. The pictures of the "nibbling of the house," of the witch as its occupant, of little Hansel behind bars, and so forth, have a disturbing effect upon the toddler and undermine his experience of "house" as such, which is for him the sole significance of the story. They would either inhibit or unfavorably accelerate the process whereby he enters into his earthly dwelling. Only when the quiet entrance into the earth-world has proceeded sufficiently and the child has attained kindergarten age can his consciousness be guided by these fairy-tale images through the difficulties that accompany the entry into life.

For toddlers it is always a boon if we can present to them a simple and untroubled image of a little house, for instance in a picture-book. For this age just the simple things and events without any story-thread work most beneficially. On approaching the kindergarten phase many toddlers will start drawing houses, perhaps with little people in them; and some parents or friends can do this in a very lively way, maybe adding here and there a little word through which the first suggestion of a story may appear. Perhaps on reaching kindergarten age a child, together with a brother or sister, may build herself a "house" under the table or with the tablecloth and a few chairs, and be completely absorbed in this activity. She will, at such an age, have an intimate experience of "house" from the fairy-tales, together with all the difficulties that have to be overcome by Hansel and Gretel.

The third theme of transition, the image of the human being, we find in almost every fairy-tale. Again the tale of Hansel and Gretel brings not only the pure image of the human being in the father, but also the depraved form of the unloving mother and the caricature of a human figure, the witch.

Strangely, contrary to reality, the element of evil generally manifests in fairy-tales in female form. How often do we not meet a witch, an evil stepmother, and so forth, beside whom the angry dwarf or giant, for instance, pales into insignificance—while the figure of the father, as here in "Hansel and

Gretel," often plays so favorable a role? For our feeling, the source of this apparent anomaly may be that the fairy-tales generally picture the soul's journey from the heavenly *Father-world* to the much harder and more demanding world of *Mother-Earth*, which to begin with presents itself as "stepmother-earth." The father would like to keep the children, but in response to the mother he must abandon them to the darkness. As for the witch, one can observe that this old, bent, and sly being represents in her nature and appearance the essential character of the difficult tests that the world of Mother Earth brings.

But quite apart from the matter of male and female, these ugly aspects of the human being disturb the utterly trusting attitude of toddlers towards humanity and darken the human image as it lives in them.

We can find many more examples of the great difference between the toddler's direct picture-experience of his surroundings, and the slightly older child's ability to absorb the no less profound but more involved and advanced picture-language of fairy-tales.

While we have brought only examples of *unfavorable* fairy-tale images—water that was enchanted, a house sheltering a witch, a "deformation" of the human image in the witch and the wicked stepmother—it should be noted that in young children's pure and uncomplicated experience of wonder towards their surroundings, even "nice" or favorable details can be confusing. All embroidering of what the child still experiences as an archetype disturbs the quiet and healthy entry of the toddler's soul into the earthly world.

6 | Materialism in the toddler and the adult

If we were to say that children cannot "rise above everyday life," or even to call them "little materialists," we would be perfectly right. But we must understand that this inability of young children to rise above ordinary things, together with their preoccupation with matter (water, sand, and so on) springs from their capacity to retain a sense of the heavenly origin of these things, which we adults no longer have. This "materialism" of the toddler, this absorption in *matter*, in Mother Earth, is in its inner aspect the opposite of the materialism of adulthood. The materialistic adult strips all matter, and also himself, of spirit; young children rediscover in their own way the spiritual principle in the things and events that surround them. If we adults were to regard this "heavenly experience of matter," this "heavenly materialism" of the toddler, as our own idea, and were able to achieve it in maturity, we would have fulfilled a part of our future tasks. Instead of stripping both ourselves and matter of spirit, we would then recognize consciously that both we and the earth are born of the spirit. We might even dimly sense or suspect future opportunities for development that go beyond merely recognizing our heavenly origin.

When the young child's "dreams of recognition" rise up again in us as adults they enable us to experience *consciously* something of the original creative forces in the world and within ourselves. The vibrant memory of water, for instance, can mean the start of a conscious relationship with the most distant past. Just now we took a step which is not yet possible for the little child, that of groping towards the future. This is what enables the grown-up to strive consciously towards the future of the world and of humanity.

In a certain sense, this heavenly, or "spiritual," materialism has for centuries been manifested in a particular way for the adult through the sacraments. Is it not so, for example, that in the sacrament of communion (that is, communion with the spirit) this connection is realized in and through the substance of bread and wine? Does not the spirit itself speak in all sacraments from the altar, through the burning candles, the vestments, and the chalice? And is not a way opened through ritual whereby higher powers may work through these substances, objects, and sacramental acts, so that their effects are received by the communicant when basic elements are brought to a living fulfilment of their essential being? In our present time, moreover, it is significant that not only the world of their origin but the forces of the future that slumber in them, the forces of the Son as well as those of the Father, can manifest and enter the soul which opens itself to them. Is not this a pure example of a spiritual materialism that points to the future?

In pre-Christian times human beings could, through initiates, renew the connection with the spirit in a hidden form by means of sacramental acts. A bridge was forged from the old relationship with the spirit to the future time when a new connection could be striven toward, after the age of spiritual darkness through which humanity would have to pass.

While the pre-Christian sacrament preserved for as long as possible the fading connection with the spirit, the Christian sacrament is an invitation and encouragement to find the new life of the spirit out of an independent mind. Young children still do this all the time, but whereas they dream themselves *back behind* the veils that hide the origin of things, adults must consciously *unveil* the forces of past and future both within ourselves and in what comes to meet us in our surroundings.

This is the future of true "materialism": the penetration of the spiritual into *mater*, Mother Earth. It is this recognition of the sense-perceptible as an expression of the spirit that enables human beings to lead themselves and the earth to their true future. The experiences of early childhood serve as a foundation for the future, and the achievements of adult life are helped or hindered by them.

If we observe the similarity between the child's experience of wonder and the adult's sacrament, we sense that they can be heard only in a mood of quiet receptivity. Just as priests cannot speak about the special qualities of the bread and wine— however true and profound their words may be—while celebrating the sacrament, so one cannot tell toddlers anything about the miracles in their surroundings which constitute their "dream-communion." In both cases it is the spirit itself which speaks its quiet language through earthly things.

We have given a couple of examples of mentioning things to very young children prematurely, such as enchanted water, where the things in themselves are not at all unfavorable. Another example may show just what the crux of the matter is.

We tell a toddler about "enchanted water" that heals all illnesses and sickness. What would be the consequence? This image is in itself not without meaning, characterizing the essence of water, so suggestive of future possibilities, and would in a fairy-tale work fruitfully for a four- or five-year-old child. But for the toddler, it would interfere with her own unprejudiced experience of water. Clearly, the step from a *direct* experience of water to hearing someone speak *about* it is an immense one. The child of kindergarten age is ripe for understanding such images and tales, but for the toddler their repetition would externalize and damage her healthy and vigorous soul-life. She would enter prematurely into the kindergarten phase—and besides "missing out" on her toddler-stage, would experience this new phase of life in a stunted form. Her natural experience of wonder, through which the heavenly gifts and attributes of his soul first enter earthly life, is cut short, while the things that she has been told about—such as the wonderful healing power of water—cannot as yet find any root in her imagination.

The manner in which children perceive all these tales, however favorable in their details, and however well-intentioned, adds to the general acceleration of their development, an increasing phenomenon of our time. Younger and younger children are taught to read and write. With prematurely logical and inartistic methods of teaching young school-children, and with ever more technical toys, there is a general drive to accelerate *external* development and a tendency to disregard the unfolding of inner gifts, which are harmed or even destroyed through acceleration. The harm done in this way is often irreparable. Each of the intimate processes with which we have been concerned can take place only at the appropriate phase of life and therefore cannot be recovered if it has been neglected, disturbed, or replaced by something essentially unsound. If in spring one picks all the blossoms from a fruit tree, the tree will not be able to replace them in the summer and will not bear fruit in autumn.

Fortunately, it is possible to observe some more positive things. We can see the recent appearance of a search for inwardness. If this search comes into its own, the wry fruits of decades of neglecting the child's inner being, fruits that we can observe clearly in our present-day society, may lose some of their bitter taste. And then, perhaps, a time of a more living understanding and guidance of what the child brings into the world may lead to more fruitful possibilities for adult life.

When children have passed undisturbed through their intimate recognition-experiences, and have been able to rediscover all that they knew in the spirit-land of their origin, and to "place" this wisdom in the sense-world that now surrounds them, then we can begin to speak to them about these wondrous encounters, and can tell of miraculous water, which has medicinal powers or has been bewitched; of the mystery house that all of a sudden seems to be made of cake; or of a human-like being who turns out to be a treacherous witch.

Of course we may begin the telling of fairy-tales before these heavenly experiences of the environment are completely over. Those children whose recognition-experiences are strongest are most receptive to fairy-tales. With their somewhat deeper nature some of this wondrous inner recognition of the sense-world remains throughout life. In the true experience of fairy-tales the initial miracle-experience lingers, just as we still hear an echo of some beautiful music when we contemplate it.

When we have allowed children's natural experience of their surroundings to ripen fully and can sense that their experience has sufficiently matured, we can gradually extend this to fairy-tales. In this way the child will be able to absorb both kinds of experience—which, after all, constitute a natural whole; and this is something that the toddler was not yet able to do.

The perception of this capacity of the child is of course a delicate matter which may not be so easy for many of us. But a clear and practical means of judging the right moment for beginning with fairy-tales can be found.

7 When is a child ready for fairy-tales?

The time when children are ready for fairy-tales and other stories is determined not only by the moment when their recognition-experiences of their surroundings have reached a certain maturity but also by their relationship to the *word*. Nature expresses itself in sounds and noises—and human beings originally did so too. For the most part they brought these forth from within, but they also imitated nature. In the course of thousands of years human speech emerged from these two sources. The process of development unfolded from a dream-experience that was purely human.

In the same way, the awakening of children out of their early dreams to an experience and an uttering of word-sounds and words is a slow business—and so it should be if their general development is to be healthy. Normally this process should be allowed to find its own rhythm. As we are unable to observe its hidden flow, we must respect its unfolding. Arbitrary intervention, especially an unwarranted hastening of the child's pace, can bring about grave disturbances in development.

Artificial word-learning—through phrases such as, "Say 'Daddy,' " "Say 'Mummy,' " "What's this?" "What's that?"—

has a wearisome and trivializing effect; for in this way children's sense of language, which should be allowed slowly to grow in a healthy manner, is awakened in an abstract, intellectual way, and with it their whole way of looking at the world. In consequence, much of the heavenly radiance children might have brought from their spiritual home is lost, becomes "crippled," or remains undeveloped, and a large part of the soul's more intimate potential is nullified.

This happens also when stories are told too early, out of a wish to accelerate verbal familiarity and comprehension. It leads to the same externalized sense of language and, therefore, to the same impoverishment. This is exacerbated in the "objective" manner of telling stories, where feeling, gesture and facial expression are suppressed and the child is forced to follow through the story conceptually through the words.

When we consider a child to be ready for fairy-tales, our story-telling must address *the whole human being* and not merely the head. We are then not expecting children to discover the story purely through the words, but are guiding them along a living experience which leads to the meaning of the fairy-tale. We should tell the tale with the facial expressions and gestures called forth by the story itself, in a manner that is free of sentimentality and "realism," for it is through these that the tale can become alive for the child.

In the land where I was born —the Dutch East Indies, as it was then—the standard for judging when a child was ready for school was whether he could reach over his head and touch his ear. Because of their larger heads and short arms, younger children are unable to do this without tilting their head to one side. Unfortunately there is no such simple little test to determine when a child is ready to follow a story.

If a child is able to follow our words well it is generally a sign that the "heavenly memories," still strongly present in the child of kindergarten age, have settled down to such an extent that he can follow a tale without disturbance. So the *natural* ability of taking in our words could be regarded as a rough way of judging when fairy-tales may be told without harm. It is much easier to observe the child's relationship to the word than the more fundamental experiences which are so deeply hidden. When the child out of himself acquires a more conscious relationship to the word, it will no longer be an effort to follow the tale, and he will no longer be so intensely related to his environment.

Such a relatively simple aid should not of course mean that our awareness of everything connected with children's inner life is not of great importance. On the contrary, the sympathy and understanding with which we are able to guide them can proceed only from such an awareness. Beginning to tell stories is deeply connected with the much wider question of the manner in which children prepare themselves for the world of fairy-tales.

Generally, a true receptivity for these begins to show itself at about the age of four. There is, however, a great difference whether we have a precociously awake child or a dreamer; or whether we are dealing with a large group of children or wishing to tell a fairy-tale intimately to one child at bedtime. Then, of course, some fairy-tales are suitable for a younger age than others.

8 Toddlers in groups with older children

The observations that have been made are, of course, most meaningful where we are concerned with one or several toddlers by themselves, as for instance in a young family. In a family or group in which there are also older children, the situation is different. The fairy-tales that one tells then are of course intended primarily for five- or six-year-olds, though an older one may come to listen too. The toddlers, for whom the tales are not intended but who happen to be around, are never personally addressed. The remarkable role which they play in this relationship is one to which we would like to give closer attention.

If we wished to "protect" the toddler we would have to tell the older children their stories at times or in places to prevent the younger ones from being there, for example in another room or when the toddlers are asleep. The former solution will not be easy, for naturally the little ones will object to this segregation! We might be able to arrange it so that when mother or grandmother is telling a fairy-tale to the older ones, father or an elder sister look after the little ones. But even that may not succeed, for when all the older ones are sitting around mother, clearly something special is happening there, and how could the toddlers not want to be there too? I don't think any father or sister will be able to stop them! Of course they may not stay for very long after finding out about those strange goings-on with which they are not really able to form a relationship. So is it really necessary to keep the toddlers so scrupulously apart?

When a toddler comes to "listen" to the fairy-tale that is being told to the older ones, she does not come to hear the content of the story, of which she has no notion, but she is irresistibly drawn to those older ones who are gathered round mother and wants to experience the special event that is happening there. Of course we do not send the child away—that would do infinitely more harm than the fairy-tale itself could ever do! But how does the child experience the story in such a case? Could it really harm her? The child hardly hears the content (which is not addressed to her). What profoundly impresses her is that all the bigger ones are coming together in a circle, that mother is telling something to which all listen, that there are word-sounds, facial expressions and gestures during the telling . . . all this works as a mystery.

This whole situation is totally different from trying to tell a fairy-tale directly to a toddler and trying to make her follow the thread of the story, which we saw as being harmful. In a larger family or mixed-age group, however, where the toddler dreamily approaches the fringe of what takes place among the older ones, this tentative approach is a natural way for her to grow into the fairy-tale circle.

Suppose we are relating a fairy-tale which tells of children being led into a dark wood where they lose their way. This image may remind us of the "preview" each of us had before birth of the "dark" earth-world to which we had to descend and in which we would initially certainly "go astray," that is to say, where the lost light of the spirit cannot immediately be found again. *We* can form for ourselves a certain conscious *thought* about this pre-earthly experience that the soul journeys through. But of course young children cannot, for they are still very much closer to the hidden inner reality of this experience, which still lives dreamily, and yet in a much more vivid way, in their souls.

Four- or five-year-olds are deeply moved by this image—which, again, is an experience of recognition, a resonance of the soul. The *resolution* of all the dark relationships in the wood and the rediscovery of the "Father-world" which is depicted by the fairy-tale can offer them a quiet confidence in their capacity in later life to find that inner light once more.

Despite their inability fully to comprehend the relevant words, toddlers have a very different experience of the image of the dark wood. In the first years of life the emphasis in the inner life is on the will to form a connection with the earthly world, and the threat of darkness and the impulse to overcome it remain completely in the background. The dark, earthly life itself is in the future; while the light of the spirit still shines through everything that happens, the earth is the promised land to which children bear their most intimate longings, and so they hardly want to be warned about it! The darkness of the earthly world is something that they must face, and they are able to do this through the great power of the light that they have brought with them. Every warning about the dangers of that earthly world at that point seems but a trifle. When the knight draws his sword against the dragon, who would then start warning him about the danger of this battle?

It will happen once in a while that a toddler, in drawing near in his mood of wonder to the fairy-tale circle, will catch from the voice, and perhaps also from the eyes, of the storyteller something of that great darkness through which every human soul must pass when it has to journey from its life in the world of spirit into the world of earthly being. It is this *human* interpretation of the darkness which, quite apart from words and story, awakens within the child a "memory." And this direct human experience without words is one which the toddler will be able to bear well, for it will not lead him away from his task of entering with heart and soul into this dark earthly-world, of uniting the riches of his soul-life with the world of earth.

A solution to the riddle of the darkness would not mean anything to him. But when these first faint experiences through the voice and facial expression of the story-teller come towards him from someone whom he can completely trust, whether parent or caregiver—this will give him all the more confidence, and even a longing, to go out to meet the darkness.

Older children of kindergarten age, already a little way within the wood, accept and are enthralled by the fairy-tale which tells how sometime in the future the light of the world will be found again. Toddlers, who with their great inner light are still confidently seeking that same darkness (and who would simply be confused by the fairy-tale's hint as to how to get *out* of it), recognize in the voice and the eyes of the storyteller their goal: the earthly darkness.

With these feelings toddlers grow slowly towards the fairy-tale circle and little by little begin to follow the words too. Then, once they have travelled further on the road to the sense-world, they will be able to enter the circle completely and receive through the words some hints as to how the light of the spirit may be rediscovered in the darkness.

We see here a completely natural development from toddler to the kindergarten phase, from an inner experience of the environment, to an absorption in the world of fairy-tales. And if we speak to the older ones freely and without prejudice, leaving the little ones to be cared for by others or to go their own way, we can trust that we have not made serious mistakes regarding the toddlers.

9 | Nursery rhymes and picture books

After the lullabies and soothing words that we offer babies, which they comprehend inwardly, we come to old and trusted games such as "Peekaboo," and nursery-rhymes like "This is the way the gentlemen ride," "Jack and Jill," and so forth. Here not only mood and content but also the sounds of the words, rhythm, and melody play an important role, and verbal comprehension is unimportant. Joining the child in play has two sides. It can be encouraging for a child when the grown-up to whom she looks up as her example in everything is absorbed in the objects of her play; yet encouragement can often be completely unnecessary, or even undesirable, as it can inhibit the child's own imagination (which is still so much more vivid than ours). Here again we must be guided by our own feelings in our search for the golden mean. Thus if a child is utterly and spontaneously absorbed in her play, obviously she should be left undisturbed; whereas if a child can play only with great difficulty, it can sometimes work beneficially if we join in with her.

A large part of the child's play consists of imitation: mother carrying the baby in her arms, father doing something in the garden, and so on. But what is there for the child truly to imitate if the adult takes a doll in his arms or hammers with a toy hammer? We are clearly concerned here with a different kind of encouragement from the deliberate example given in the course of play. Sitting together on chairs and making the sounds of a cart, or a train in a tunnel, will be more effective. The same goes for floating a little boat on the water or building a little house together out of blocks.

Even when we do not participate in or encourage their play, our interest in children is vital. In play, the heavenly aspect of the child's being unites with the earthly world; and if we have an open eye and an open heart for this, children feel it—and that brings confidence to help them on their way.

What children hear of *words* and *word-sounds* and the way that they begin very slowly to understand them is particularly significant. To begin with, of course, we do not intend to convey information. What we offer are sounds of caress and sympathy, and when we notice that a child begins to understand a little of what we say, it is important that we do not expect an immediate understanding of our words. As we observed, this would only awaken children from dream-experiences that they still need. It would make them "deaf" to what their surroundings have to impart to them, without which healthy development is impossible.

Yet we should not deny young children our intimate words and "little tales." Children need our sympathetic voice and word-sounds no less than the "songs without words" from their surroundings. Just as an infant would languish without our soothing words and lullabies, and as a baby would suffer inwardly without our nursery-rhymes and little games, a toddler would not thrive without our words and word-sounds that harmonize with his tender experiences. But how can we let him hear these? What does this age demand of us?

Through the sound of gentle words, the first dreamy consciousness of language grows in childhood. But after the songs that we always sung in the time of babyhood, and after the little words that we have spoken, it gradually becomes right that children enter into the impressions of their surroundings and into what they themselves can do there. We can express our interest through the running of water from a tap into a bowl and the floating of boats and blocks, through what a doll says who is allowed out of bed again, and so on.

Two things are of particular importance. First, the child senses—initially perhaps only through our mood and without our speaking about it—how we, too, live in the things and events that surround him. Children's intimate search for an entrance to the earthly world through absorption in his surroundings is guided and strengthened when they can experience how important these things are also for us. We should not in any way force our sympathy on them, but we will quietly be able to help them in their endeavor to regain an experience (now conscious) of the non-material source of the things that surround us. The rushing and flowing of water, the experience of being carried by the solid little boat through this transparent fluid, the human being as expressed by the doll, all these must become like miracles for us once more, in a modest but real way. The rediscovery of this world in us can—without our noticing it—extend a hand to the child immersed in his own world of experiences.

The second point is that children also long to hear the mystery of human speech. Together with what their surroundings speak to them, they can experience the unity formed by these two aspects of their experience. We should—without disturbing what the children themselves perceive—allow them at suitable moments to hear our human words, so that these may join in an intimate dialogue with the language of the surroundings.

The point here is that both our human language and the silent language of things proceed from that same inaudible heavenly world, and therefore they have to develop together. Our awareness of this can work in a helpful way for the toddler.

To take the example of water running into a bowl, we should let this gushing speak so that children can take in that language in all its purity and recognize it inwardly. Then without making too much of it, we can at another time let them hear clearly the *sh*-sound and the word *gush*. Children can then experience the extent to which we human beings even in our language carry the whole world within us and are ourselves a microcosm of that world. When we are walking in the garden and then speak the word *tree* and maybe also the word *rustling*, a child will find a proper connection with this only if in these sounds she hears something of what the rustling tree has first spoken to her. In this way it is possible for the child to experience through our words an inner connection between the language of things and human language.

It is better if we do not begin by speaking *about* the things in the child's environment but rather leave these to speak for themselves, for if this is done in a natural and responsible manner it can strengthen an inward listening in the child. We can, perhaps let the child hear the doll *itself* say "Good morning," and then answer this greeting. We can "hear" the push-chair announce that it so likes to carry little Lucy and wants to roll along with her on it, and so on. In these "messages" that bring to children stories in human words about their surroundings, we address toddlers in a true language.

In these "tales of interpretation" they can live and rediscover their surroundings in us, and can find us in their surroundings; this is one of the most important conditions for their development at this stage.

Only when children have become a little more independent from their surroundings can communications *about* things and *about* people be made, as for instance in fairy-tales. And when this has come about, the toddler has begun to tread the earth with confidence, and is now ready for kindergarten.

When we look quietly at a picture-book with a child we can in the most natural and unforced way combine image, movement, sound, facial expression, and many other aspects, in a harmonious whole. This is of the greatest importance for the connection between the language of things and our spoken language.

But the picture-book has another quality that can be of particular importance. Through it all that has already approached children is brought to them, and speaks to them anew in the language of pictures, but now as expressed by human beings. This is akin to the way a painter can teach us to "see" something, for instance through a beautiful landscape—we see it through him and with him. The child now sees and feels that he does not stand alone in his meetings and experiences with his surroundings. He will feel welcomed and understood by us through looking at a picture-book, for he tries to become still more strongly aware of the adult's sense of oneness with his world.

With this in mind there should be no reason whatsoever to think that dwelling upon the most normal, everyday things should have a narrowing or trivializing effect. On the contrary, we saw that it is just these "normal" things which have the greatest and most important messages to impart, for they bring to expression the simplest and most fundamental aspects of life on earth.

Accordingly, the picture-book for the toddler should depict the simplest things and the most ordinary actions. Unusual things and events work in a distracting and confusing way. And for the same reasons that the fairy-tale is not suitable for the toddler, the pictures should not yet have a story-thread. Here again the things and actions simply speak their own language out of their own true being and purpose. There is a sincere longing to bring the child what is good and appropriate, but every now and then we come across some absurd tomfoolery created without regard to a child's nature or age: for example, a duck with a turned-up beak, cheeky waving wings and a sailor's cap, or a hippopotamus with rolling eyes and a top-hat askew on one ear. In this way, the sense-world—which in its very simplicity is a realm of mystery for the child—is portrayed as a trivial farce.

It will hardly need explaining why these images from which the child has no means of protecting himself have a detrimental effect on his pure relationship to the visible world and may even do subtle permanent damage. If the harm inflicted has penetrated so far that the child responds to this "fun," it is no proof of the childlike quality of the "humor" but rather of the child's vulnerability in trustfully accepting everything that the adult brings him, and letting himself be led completely astray by this vulgarity.

Something that may appeal to our healthy sense of humor may not be suitable for the little child. Despite all her cheerfulness, the tiniest toddler cannot relate to the business of laughing at foolishness. Such a child can laugh merrily if you make fun of yourself, for instance in a game of peekaboo. She may also laugh if mother and father are fooled and pull a funny face for her, and she can laugh when another person laughs. To some extent she has her own little jokes, but she cannot laugh objectively at an absurd drawing. At most she will, as I have frequently experienced, say something like "That's funny, isn't it?"—an implication of rejection.

It is a joy that the child cannot yet laugh at anything so banal. Laughing at a grotesquely depicted object means that one has, like the artist, finished with the thing as a wholeness and is now placing oneself over against it: one judges it, and laughs at it. And that is just what goes against the nature of toddlers, who enter fully into everything through their dreamy recognition-experiences. If this possibility is taken from them and they are forced to laugh at an absurd representation of what they have recognized on so deep a level, this leads them to the desecration and denial of what is most precious in their souls.

These false impressions live in the unconscious and can surface later, for instance in a desire to mock every serious quest for spiritual values. In a wider context, this may lead to a loss of those feelings of reverence which are a foundation for all spiritual development.

Only when the toddler approaches kindergarten age does he have the first inkling of a sense for what is really funny in such a drawing. An appreciation develops for an amusing event that is depicted: for instance, someone hurrying to be first who slips and falls on his bottom, a child who wants to have sweets but finds instead something bitter in his mouth, and so on. Comic situations of this kind are the beginnings of a story-thread, which leads from what things themselves have to say to a story about things.

We see that the real significance of the picture-book for toddlers is that they find in it a portrayal of everything that has resonated in their inner being, created by adults with dedication and respect.

I have little sympathy for picture-books composed of children's drawings for children. A child's drawing is inspired by observation, sometimes even in great detail, and yet its deeper source lies in the world of dream-experience. This inspiration descends from above, which is why they can be so interesting for us. But as young children are themselves making this "descent" from the dream-world, they long for something to be brought towards them that enables them to recognize the things from their surroundings: they long to meet with certainties rather than seek what also is still descending. It is therefore essential that the picture-book be drawn or painted by an adult, one who is able to enter to some extent into the heavenly world of the toddler. Then the pictures can offer young children a trust that their inner treasures will be rediscovered when they themselves have grown into this adult-world.

10 | Story-thread and language for the toddler

A good picture-book, one that depicts cheerfully and without a story the simplest things and actions, will help us to find a healthy way of "interpreting" the pictures for the toddler. We can simply let him see and hear what the picture itself wishes to portray; for instance: "This is a man . . . and this man is chopping," and we can make gestures to accompany this sound: "Chop, chop, chop! He is chopping wood." Later, perhaps after several months, we can connect these three thoughts thus: "This man is chopping wood, chop, chop, chop!" Inevitably an event or action, however insignificant, contains a first little tale. But it is the *action* that is emphasized rather than the things. Similarly we can proceed from images like "woman," "pump," "water," to "This woman pumps water," again with gestures and emphasizing sounds.

Most of the time we quite naturally carry out this "interpreting" of a particular picture with the same intonation, gestures and sounds. This repetition is good for the child. He feels profoundly connected with our presentation which is indeed a miniature "incarnation process" for him: his soul finds embodiment in these sounds and gestures. Constant change would have a disturbing and disquieting effect. We shall often be reprimanded if we do it "wrongly," that is, differently from previous occasions. "No!" I once was told off, "No, not chop, chop. Chop, chop, chop!" Indeed a great difference! We are not even allowed to alter the words. If we have once spoken of "wood," we may not on the next occasion say "logs."

We may still observe this characteristic in the four or five-year-old, and we shall have to bear it in mind when we repeat fairy-tales, for example. There, too, we should not introduce any changes into the chosen words or into the facial expressions and gestures with which the child has formed a connection.

Many of us will be able to remember how wonderful it was and how good it felt to have the same words and gestures repeated again and again. We looked forward to what was to come, and grew into it when the moment duly arrived: the dark voice in the dark wood, the croaking voice of the witch, or the quacking of the little white duck. Only later can the child develop a little more independence from these earliest embodiments of his soul-life.

Now when the first signs of a sense for stories have begun to show in the toddler, we can start very gradually to take these things further—even though the fuller development of this faculty comes only with the five-year-old. Continuing with the given examples and keeping to the same pictures and the same voice, facial expression, and gesture, we would be able to say, for instance: "This man chops wood for his wife: chop, chop, chop! Now the woman pumps water, sh-sh-sh! And here" (next picture) "she lights a fire, ff-ff-ff! And now" (another picture, though every picture should of course be looked at quietly for a long time) "she hangs the pan of water above the fire until the water boils, bubble, bubble, bubble!" and so on. Like this we make a quite natural and gradual transition—which should not be too quick—from the sounds of words to their meaning and a simple story.

We can, so as to keep the first impressions completely pure and unmixed, also take other picture-books—and select those in which a certain coherence of narrative begins to appear: two little ducks that go out walking and swimming and have all sorts of adventures; a little boy who goes picking blueberries, and so forth, until finally the child of kindergarten age can be told fairy-tales.

While the story is told it is possible for the child to look at the pictures. In a larger group, for instance in a play-group, this is obviously not often practicable. But here it is particularly important to allow the older ones the opportunity of freely developing their imagination. However, at home with one or two little children of this age, we can look at pictures during the fairy-tale, provided that they are really beautiful and speak to the child's world of dreams. I recall vividly an illustration by Gustave Doré of the entry of Tom Thumb's family into the dark wood, father in front with his big axe, which called forth experiences which have played a part throughout my life. The children should not look at the pictures after the story is told, for otherwise they will have already formed their own imaginations which would be disturbed or replaced by the pictures from the book.

It should be stressed that our own feelings and experience should guide our looking at the picture-book, and telling stories to children. One point to watch, especially with the youngest toddlers, is that we do not look at too many pictures one after the other. This is because a surfeit of images disturbs the quiet intimacy that belongs with each picture. Then, as each picture-book breathes a completely different atmosphere, looking at more than one book at a time may have a confusing effect especially at bedtime. So it would seem good that we restrict ourselves to one picture-book which can then bring a mood of total peace and dedication.

It is also good if in the course of some days we look again and again at the same picture-book, just as later we tell the same fairy-tale over and over again. This helps the development of a profound relationship with the pictures, and later to the fairy-tale. Thus we should regard it as a good and healthy sign if the child asks—even for weeks at a time—for the same picture-book or fairy-tale. This shows how deeply he experiences what he takes in, and we should satisfy this longing. Just as in a religious service for adults the repetition of certain words and actions makes for the deepest effect, so impressions of the pictures and fairy-tale images become ever more intimate and deeply rooted. We shall also be able to observe the extent to which joy in repetition grows continually and how healthily this works on the inner growth of the child.

Unfortunately there are few picture-books which are really good for the toddler, allowing both the things and the simple events of life to speak for themselves, and as yet having no story-thread. There are plenty of illustrated fairy-tales and other stories, but books with pictures for the toddler are few and far between. If we look with the child of this age at the same books over and over again, there is no need for a large number of books.

However, if these cannot be found, one possibility is that we do the drawings ourselves, preferably while we are telling the story and with the child watching. Of course many people think—"Oh, I can't do that at all and I couldn't learn it either!"

There are, however, more possibilities than most of us think. The point is, after all, that through our simple sketches we awaken the imagination and sympathy of the child. And if we draw with faith and without heaviness, not wishing to do it better than we are able, we shall often feel that it works like magic. I cannot draw at all, and yet the child is fascinated—it is as if miracles are born from my fingers.

What fascinates children is not how well we can draw but the fact that our scribbles, which they imbue with their own fantasy, call forth their inner recognition-experiences. Through this, toddler's longing for the earthly world will be awakened in a more lively manner than through any picture-book, and in the same way their trust in being truly understood and able to find their way in life will be strengthened. There are many clever artists and painters, and there are many who are clumsy but who nevertheless are able to offer children exactly what they need, having the ability to awaken their memories of the world from which they came.

However inadequate the adult's sketches may be from an artistic point of view, they bring something which a child's picture does not have. This is a certainty that the nature of the child's quest for the earthly world is understood by the adult.

And when adults try to open themselves to the source of the child's soul and to share in that longing to enter into earthly life, then they will be able to offer children what they are looking for.

It is our conviction that starting from this respect for things and this love for the child, almost every adult would be capable of bringing children what they need in this realm.

For instance, say slowly, drawing at the same time: "Look,

this is Mother knitting by the fire, and this is Puss playing with a ball of wool; Father is feeding the dog and Rachel is watering the plants," and so on, so that all that happens there, and also every person, every object—the ball of wool, the knitting-needles, the watering-can—speaks its own language. That is what is important for the toddler.

Another possibility is that we manage to find picture-books which come as close as possible to the goal that we set and which we then describe, omitting the narrative-content. We simply relate what we see, without making too much of it, and we speak our words calmly and clearly: "There swims Mother-duck with her ducklings: quack, quack, quack, peep, peep, peep!" For the slightly older ones we can embellish our interpretation a little, as we did with the man and the woman: "Look, there swims Mother-duck with all her ducklings and Mother-duck says: 'Quack, quack quack, little children, are you all here?'—'Peep, peep, peep, yes mother, we are all here!' " and so on. In this way we leave out the actual story.

And when we turn to a new picture—unless the child does this himself—we need not begin immediately with the interpretation, but may first allow time for what is there to speak itself, and offer the child the opportunity to take everything in calmly. This should be done also every time the picture is looked at again. Then after this period of undisturbed looking, we may begin a little conversation about it, which the child or we may start, and in this way the things can begin to express themselves also in our words.

Thus everyone will be able to find the best way of avoiding or removing the unnecessary thread of narrative for the toddler.

Once my grandson, a young toddler, managed to do that

through his own highly original initiative. He was with his older brother (also still a toddler) on my lap, and we all were looking at a picture-book, a version of a fairy-tale and thus not really suitable for toddlers. It had caught his attention because of its beautiful colors, and, as it was taken out of the cupboard by the eldest brother, I had no wish to disapprove and preferred, rather, to try to look at it in toddler fashion. But through my attention being concentrated on the elder who was nearly of kindergarten age, little bits of the story kept creeping in. The little one would not accept this, and his solution—which I would never have thought of—was suddenly to turn over six or eight pages at once, then ten back, and so forth. This was precisely the help that I needed to keep completely to the picture itself and to abandon all story.

The brother was entirely content with this, even though he would have been able to cope with something of a story. Later I heard that the two had been looking at picture-books in this way also at home, with the younger brother taking care how the pages were turned and the elder giving his commentary about every picture that happened to fall open. Thus we can use any book with simple and beautiful pictures for toddlers.

For the little child it must be a curious experience in his early years to discover how people address one another with words. We should once put ourselves in his place. He observes how, through word-sounds, people create a certain relationship with one another. When one person has uttered some of these strange sounds, the other answers him with some more. The meaning of these sounds remains hidden from the child. He understands the things around him without the help of words, but the word-sounds of people he does not comprehend. Speech itself is to him a world rich in mystery, but the words themselves cannot yet reveal their meaning. Through divergence into many tongues and through the development of the intellect, their sounds have moved so far from their source that they can no longer be recognized. Because of this, the meaning of ordinary human words—for all the fascination and effectiveness of their sounds—is for the time being unknown territory for the child.

But certain words—like "spray," for example—do give us an experience through their sound of what such a thing does. Other examples are words that we have already mentioned: water, stream, dash (as of waves), roar (as of the sea), murmur (as of a stream), wind; all of which express in their sounds something of their meaning and of what happens. These onomatopoeic words are best for the little child, and we should show them to their best advantage through a clear and natural pronunciation. Poets, too, will often express themselves in their sound-paintings through these words.

Examples of this sort are common, but unfortunately are usually spoken carelessly and only seldom come to prominence. This externalization, this dull and sloppy daily use of the spoken word, is the chief reason why the step from the imaginative-experience of his surroundings to the understanding of human language is so great and so far-reaching for the young child. It is the step from an inner participation in the phenomena to a more external intellectual understanding: an inevitable process. Nevertheless, so far as we are able we should fashion healthy forms by speaking as calmly and naturally as possible through the living sounds of the words. A curious and important part is played here by sound-expressions such as jingles and nursery-rhymes, where the inevitable first beginnings of a story-element are rendered "harmless" through being made so delightfully nonsensical; here word-sounds can come to the fore in a lively way. Remember how we used to delight in nursery rhymes, such as "Humpty-Dumpty sat on the wall," and "Hickety, pickety, my red hen," and "Eeny, meeny, miny, mo." The playfully childish content is ushered in "on a bed of sound," and despite the narrative element that is prominent in some of these, a melody can further strengthen this living and dreaming into the sounds.

These nursery-rhymes and play-songs have the great virtue of being able to help the child to bring into the intellectual realm of present-day human language the rich picture-language of things and actions, adorned with sound, melody, and nonsense and allowing it to live on afterwards beneath the surface. They protect the child from too early an external understanding of words, preserving the mystery of the sounds. They are the sacraments of the little child, in the sense that where Communion helps us to regain the spiritual element in our earthly environment, the "sacrament" of the nursery-rhyme helps the child from early on in life to guide the spirit into the very heart of his existence.

11 Imitation

One important characteristic, indispensable for the child, is the inborn desire to imitate. Now that the search for earthly existence has been fulfilled through being born on the earth, the child recognizes in each of his elders one whose guidance and example he will follow with trust and devotion. Older brothers and sisters will also be closely imitated in many of their usual activities by the little child.

The posture, gesture and facial expression of grown-ups is sometimes adopted, though the child is of course not conscious of doing this. Even moral posture, which is so inward and hidden, is formed according to our example, with the result that the character of our actions, our voice, and our glance makes a profound impression on children. We become aware that bringing up children is done not merely through word and deed but to a great part also through our inner attitudes, and with the youngest children this is still of the greatest importance.

In the first years of life, imitation is one of the most important functions that the child performs; only afterwards does what has been imitated acquire a character of its own and more and more new things are independently learned and fashioned.

One of the clearest examples of the abilities children acquire through imitation is speech. They would not be able to learn this at all without the example of their elders. Through the dreamy, yet wholly dedicated imitation of the sounds of words children learn to speak their mother tongue. We know that we should not hasten or force the growth of this imitation process but, as with all important developments, allow it to come to fulfillment in its own time.

When the little toddler begins to seek the passage from the picture-language of things to the language of words, and tries to connect these with each other, the picture-book can be of considerable help. When we look quietly at the book while interpreting it in word, sound and gesture, and enter into the child's questions with intimate understanding, this, instead of hurrying the child on, will enhance a truly calm possibility of taking the step from the language of the world to the language of human beings.

This was shown to me in a delightful way by my two little grandchildren. It had become a habit that whenever they visited us the elder—with the younger soon following his example—immediately fetched a picture-book from our cupboard and laid it on my knee. The highly meaningful word, "book," was then spoken, and this meant: "You are going to look at this book with us!" Then I had to take the two on my lap, one on each knee, and share experiences of the things that were to be seen, doing all this slowly, with voice and gesture insofar as there was still an arm available:

"This is a farmer."

"What is a farmer, Grandpa?"

"A farmer is a man who works the land," (making an appropriate gesture) "but this farmer is letting his horse drink. The horse drinks water out of a trough. Look how nicely the horse drinks: slosh, slosh, slosh! and the farmer lays his hand on the shoulder of the horse. . ." and so on in the same vein.

Not all the words need to be understood, as it is primarily the pictures that matter; the main point is that the sounds of the words are heard. All this was taken in with quiet attention, or at any rate it was either dreamily or merrily repeated after me. And if I forgot something, the elder brother would grab my finger and point to what I had left out, so that this too would have its proper turn and was properly imitated. The children showed clearly how everything, and particularly all that is familiar, had to be said and done by me as an adult, and how they were utterly absorbed in imitating, either inwardly or audibly and visibly.

This merry but deeply serious entry by way of picture and sound into a world which for these toddlers is endlessly new and also intimately familiar can give one the feeling of going together with a child through something very special: the child takes another silent step into earthly life, bearing all the wealth that has brought with him.

The same picture-books were almost always chosen; only rarely was another book laid on my lap, and this would generally offer something to look at which could captivate the attention in the best sense of the word. Once, unexpectedly, a biography of Rudolf Steiner was pressed into my hand. "Book!" made it clear what had to be done. I did not have the time to find another, for the eldest brother had on this occasion immediately begun with his commentary about the cover, on which were to be seen several clear colors which had apparently attracted him: "Good, lellow," it sounded from his little mouth; and when we opened the book we soon came across a picture of the first Goetheanum. "This," I said, after a brief period of quiet attention, "is a big house, a very big house. And here you go up the stairs in front of the house: step, step, step. Then you come into a great hall, into a very great hall," and so on. Then there was a portrait of Rudolf Steiner as a young man. "This is a man," I said. "Man," was imitated. In the end the children were deeply content and I had the feeling that we had been looking at a very good picture-book for this age.

When children have, until the age of four, absorbed without hindrance the revelations of the earthly world and have ever and again experienced the feeling of wonder as they recognize what they behold, the phase of speaking *about* what is observed may slowly proceed. Until this time it was always a great miracle to meet in sense-perceptible form what was already present within. Now it is possible to bring children *elaborations* of what they perceive, in the form of fairy-tales: these would only confuse the toddlers, but through their picture-language they give children of kindergarten age an experience of the connections that exist between their own development and that of the world.

As we have been concerned here with the transition from toddler to kindergarten age and have become convinced that the toddler is not yet ready for fairy-tales, it is interesting to note Maria Montessori's complete ban on fairy-tales. Montessori rejects these tales for *all* young children on the grounds that one may bring only "the truth," by which she means *outer* sense-perceptible reality.

We do not need to point out here that a conception of this kind can only proceed from a complete denial of the great truths and directives that are expressed by the fairy-tales in their own language and which can be so profoundly meaningful to children if offered at the right age and in the right way. With regard to the toddler, however, we agree with Montessori in that for children of this age, we should confine ourselves to bringing only sense-perceptible realities. But in contrast to one who regards as reality only its outer aspect and who thereby denies every deeper truth which may be concealed therein, we hold that every earthly reality itself reveals its heavenly origin to the little child. We therefore regard the so-called "limitation" to earthly realities, where toddlers are concerned, as a great expansion, a protection of the heavenly sphere which they continue to recognize.

12 The transition from toddler to young child

As a starting point in grasping the essential transition from toddler to kindergarten-age child we may take an example that appeared in our earlier discussion as one of the more intimate aspects of his relationship to his environment. For a toddler every tranquil perception of a house, whether it be a real house, in a picture, or in her play or toys, points imperceptibly to the "house" of her own soul, her body, and in this way a dreamy memory is awakened of the time when her soul took possession of this body-house. Through this hidden experience, the incarnation-process of the child, which is still taking place, is strongly influenced in a calming way. It is for this reason that the quiet impression, "house," ought not—in whatever way it is awakened in the child—to be robbed of its original simplicity through adding superfluous details. The toddler still lives in the archetypal phenomenon, which reveals itself to her inner being; and she must be able to give himself up to this in tranquility and without hindrance.

For a child of kindergarten age, however, who has journeyed a little further on her path of incarnation, the seeing and experiencing of a house can no longer be regarded merely as a desirable support for this process: she longs for answers to the questions that slumber in her about what will come towards her in the house where she has begun her own life and what she will herself have to do there.

It is answers to these questions which fairy-tales bring to the child of kindergarten age. And here a completely new element makes itself felt, for the fairy-tale cannot give these answers without venturing beyond the reality of the sense-world. For toddlers, the *things* that are seen (for instance the house) are at the same time the *images* of their heavenly counterparts. The house proceeds from the same soul-enveloping archetype as the body. This picturing faculty, which echoes a pre-earthly past, is still present, though in a greatly diminished form, in children of kindergarten age, but they focus their attention no less upon the future.

That is why the fairy-tale must reach beyond observation of the sense-world. It must, for instance, describe how Hansel and Gretel nibble the little house that they find in the wood, how they then come under the power of the witch who inhabits it; and finally how, on vanquishing her, they are carried over the river by a white swan (sometimes referred to as a white duck) and on the other side find the "Father-world" again. Here is the soul, standing in earthly life before temptations and dangers and yet battling with them, which after going through darkness finally finds the light of the spirit once more. Only through these pictures which transcend the realm of the senses, and which would be both meaningless and disturbing for the toddler, can the fairy-tale bring to children of kindergarten age what they need as an inner foretaste of life to come.

So we see that the transition from toddlerhood to kindergarten age means, in fact, the step from the heavenly past to the (as yet) dream-enshrouded future. For toddlers, the memory of the soul's entry from the spiritual world into the body requires a faithfulness to the images of the sense-world which call these memories forth. With children of kindergarten age, these representations must be elaborated and amplified in order that the future may be brought in picture-form towards them and towards all that they have to do and experience; the fairy-tale that is to depict this must of necessity overstep the bounds of the sense-perceptible. The transition out of toddlerhood is a step out of the pure experience of the surroundings into absorption in the fairy-tale world.

When, earlier on, we suggested certain yardsticks for judging the child's readiness for the world of fairy-tales, we stressed that these should not be regarded as dogmas. Similarly, we trust that all other observations will be understood in such a way as to allow freedom. This applies also to the suggestion that where toddlers are concerned we should confine ourselves to sense-perceptible realities.

To avoid misunderstandings, let us look at the following. Everyone who has a healthy relationship to little children will surely love to see them playing with an old-fashioned hobby-horse. How great is the significance of the hobby-horse, especially for the child of kindergarten age. And how good it is to see children—first the four- or five-year-old and then, timidly imitating, also the toddler—ride the hobby-horse. And how strongly we may feel in both cases that this is particularly good for them. How are we to understand this, and how does it tally with our observations? It is, after all, a gross violation of the visible form of the horse if a simple stick represents the whole body.

We should first of all realize that nothing has been added to the body of our hobby-horse—the point is, rather, that a lot has been left out. Through this, nothing is forced on to the child. And then the mane-covered head of the horse often works so strongly on the imagination that this, quite of itself, is able to fill in the missing part of the body with the result that the child's inner formative powers are strengthened.

Thus we see that these early developmental phases of the child, demanding all that they do from us by way of consciousness, understanding and guidance, are too subtle in nature and too richly differentiated to be fitted into rigid rules or laws. Each of us will have to develop for ourselves our own sympathy with the child, and out of that a real ability both to see and to act, taking each case on its own merits.

One of our most essential tasks is to listen sympathetically to what the earth, at once so new and yet so intimately familiar, would divulge to the child. While the fairy-tale presents to children of kindergarten age the picture-clad assurance that they may, as adults, eventually be able to rise above the shackles of earthly relationships, so does Mother Earth in her intimate way show still smaller children, rediscovering in all that surrounds them, the miracle of the embodiment of their own being in her realm. Thus the revelations of Mother Earth and the promise of the fairy-tale move in opposite directions: the former leads earthwards, the latter points heavenwards; and both thereby fulfil their essential task.

And yet both soul-journeys, are, despite their contrary direction, related. The embodiment of the toddler's soul-life in the things of the earthly world is in itself an uplifting event. The toddler's memory-experiences of the heavenly world are an imperceptible reaching back to the beginnings of spiritual life on earth. And what the fairy-tale presents to the older child as an ideal that will one day be realized consciously, namely, the redemption of the earthly-world from its darkness, is already fulfilled in a dreamy way by the toddler. The first foundations for the fulfilment of this great task of the adult are laid not in the kindergarten child, but in the toddler. We could say that as adults we would hardly be able to attain to the fullest realization of this great task of rediscovering the spirit on earth if we had not been allowed in our earliest years to dream in this twofold way.

For children of kindergarten age this dream is of the future, and we make this dreaming possible by telling them fairy-tales. Toddlers find other fulfillment in all that the things around whisper to them, for it is through this that they unknowingly unite their own secrets with those of the earthly world. And if we can only experience a little of the dream-mystery which has been entrusted to the very young, we will offer them a fruitful environment manifesting the pure elements of this world and bearing witness to a pure, practical humanness. Then they can enter earthly life with all their heavenly gifts in such a way that they will later discover these gifts consciously in the world.

The "dream-mystery" that toddlers thus observe around them is the great open secret of Mother Earth—the mystery which, although we do not immediately comprehend it, she entrusts to the young child in her whispering way.

About the author

Daniel Udo de Haes was born in 1899 into a family with six children in Bali, Indonesia (then under Dutch colonial rule). In his ninth year, the family moved to Holland. Daniel studied physics and mathematics at Leiden University and became a teacher in the Hague. He then went to Zeist and encountered the Anthroposophy of Rudolf Steiner, which inspired all his further work.

At a conference he met his future wife, Johanna van Goudover, with whom he had three children. In Zeist, he taught in a Waldorf elementary school, and then worked until his retirement as a teacher in an anthroposophic institute for children with special needs, "Het Zonnehuis."

Toward the end of this period he wrote, illustrated, and self-published a series of books for young children, *Zonnegeheimen*, containing tales, fables and small poems. After his retirement he also wrote a series of educational books for parents and teachers. A focus of his work was the importance of telling the traditional fairy tales to young children. He continued with these educational writings up to his death in March, 1986, in Zeist.

About the translation

WECAN is pleased to be able to bring this classic work back into print nearly thirty years after its original publication in English. We are grateful to Floris Books for permission to use the original translation as the basis for a new, revised edition.

An explanatory note to this translation read, "The translation has been made freely to suit the different culture of the English-speaking countries, omitting some references to particularly Dutch uses, and occasionally adding a few sentences as, for instance, Wordsworth's famous verses in Chapter One." In addition, for this new edition we have attempted to give a more balanced treatment of the two genders. We hope that a new generation will find within these pages many treasures for study, as well as active working and living with young children.

Other WECAN books you will enjoy:

Other WECAN books you will enjoy:

Tell Me a Story
Stories from the Waldorf Early Childhood Association of North America
Edited by Louise deForest

Contributed by members and friends of WECAN, over 80 of our favorite stories for all ages and all occasions. **$25**

The Wilma Ellersiek Gesture Games Series:
Giving Love—Bringing Joy
Gesture Games for Spring and Summer
Gesture Games for Autumn and Winter
Dancing Hand—Trotting Pony

A bounteous feast of life-giving song, movement and gesture. **Each volume $28**

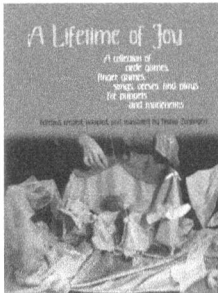

A Lifetime of Joy
A Collection of Circle Games, Finger Games, Songs, Verses and Plays
Bronja Zahlingen

A treasure trove of nourishment is found in this collection that Bronja gathered over many years of work with children and the adults who care for them. **$18**

845-352-1690 • information@waldorfearlychildhood.org
store.waldorfearlychildhood.org

.

www.ingramcontent.com/pod-product-compliance
Lightning Source LLC
Chambersburg PA
CBHW052141270326
41930CB00012B/2978